Batting Against the Odds

Written by Lynette Evans
Illustrated by Marjorie Scott

North America

Contents

Who Was Jackie Robinson?

Jackie Robinson was a famous African American athlete. He was the first person to break through the barriers that allowed only Americans with white skin to play baseball in the major leagues during the early to mid-1900s.

Jackie Robinson is admired not only for his great skill as a baseball player but also for the bravery, patience, and self-control he showed when others treated him unfairly and cruelly.

1919	1920	1930s	1945
Jackie is born in Albany, Georgia, the youngest of five children.	Jackie's mother moves with the children to California.	Jackie is a champion athlete and is accepted at the University of California, Los Angeles.	Jackie becomes the first African American to play in the major leagues.

U.S.A. before the 1960s

Although slavery was made illegal in 1863, African Americans were still treated unfairly, especially in the South, where Jackie Robinson was born.

African Americans were forced to ride in separate areas on trains and buses, eat in separate restaurants, and sleep in separate hotels from white people. They went to separate schools and churches and often held the lowest-paying jobs. New laws were passed in the 1960s that made it illegal to treat people differently because of their race.

CANADA

Montreal

U.S.A.

Pasadena, California

Albany, Georgia

1946	1947–56	1956–63	1972
Jackie marries his college sweetheart, Rachel Isum. They eventually have three children.	Jackie breaks the colour barrier in sports, paving the way for other black players.	Jackie retires from baseball but continues to campaign for civil rights across America.	Jackie dies as a result of suffering from diabetes for many years.

5

Westward Bound

*Mallie Robinson forced herself to remain calm
while the policeman checked her train tickets
and rudely kicked the suitcases and boxes
that were piled at the side of the track.*

*Her youngest child, Jack, slept in her arms,
weary after the long buggy ride from
the farm. The four older children waited
nervously. At last, the family was allowed
to board the segregated train. They left
Georgia and began their long journey
west to a new life in California.*

segregated   divided into separate sections
because of skin colour

6

Jack Roosevelt Robinson was the youngest of five children. His father, Jerry Robinson, worked on a large farm in Georgia. When Jerry left his wife and children, Mallie Robinson decided to move her family to California. Life had become violent and dangerous for many African Americans living in the South, and Mallie had heard about the promise of a better life in the West.

Mallie Robinson is shown here with her children (from left): Mack, Jack, Edgar, Willa Mae, and Frank.

The Little Mother

"Come on, Jackie, we'll be late for school,"
Willa Mae said to her baby brother. When Mallie
found a job as a maid, she gave each of her older
children the responsibility of looking after the next
younger child. So Willa Mae bathed, dressed, and
fed Jackie almost every day. He even went to school
with her and was allowed to play outside in the
sandbox while she sat in class and watched him
through a window.

responsibility being trusted with something

Mallie Robinson arrived in California with only three dollars sewn into the lining of her clothes. She found a job as a maid for a white family in Pasadena and worked long hours.

At first, times were tough, and the children sometimes went hungry. After a while, however, Mallie had saved enough money to buy a house. The family grew their own fruit and vegetables.

Jackie's mother's house on Pepper Street, Pasadena, California

Odd Ones Out

"Jackie, take that energy of yours outside and do some chores," Mallie Robinson said gently to her eight-year-old son, who always seemed to be running, jumping, and playing ball.

Jackie began to sweep the sidewalk outside their house on Pepper Street. Suddenly, the little girl across the street screamed at him, "Get out of our neighbourhood! We don't want to see your black face around here!"

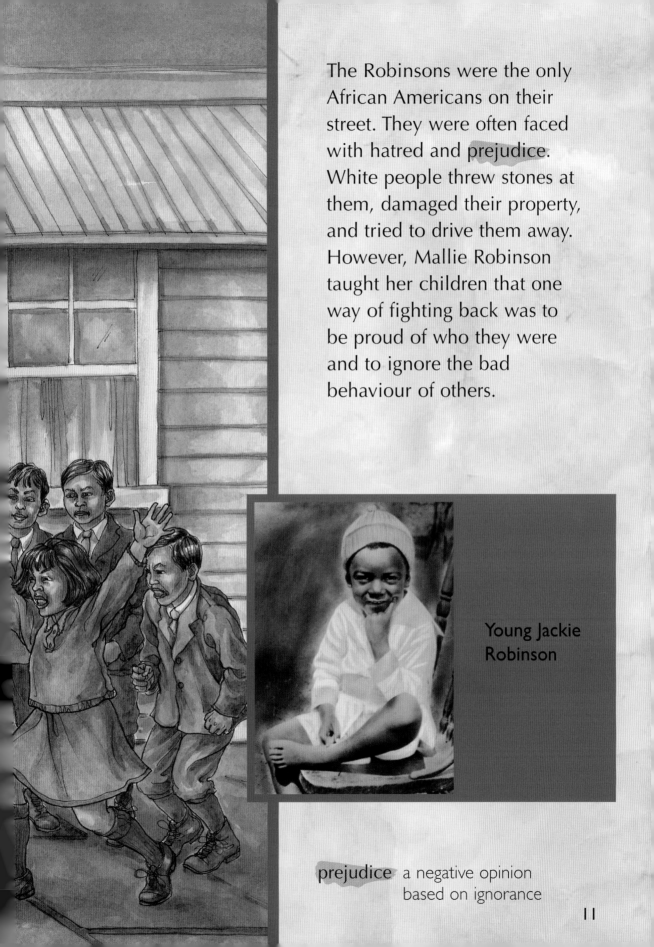

The Robinsons were the only African Americans on their street. They were often faced with hatred and prejudice. White people threw stones at them, damaged their property, and tried to drive them away. However, Mallie Robinson taught her children that one way of fighting back was to be proud of who they were and to ignore the bad behaviour of others.

Young Jackie Robinson

prejudice a negative opinion based on ignorance

That's Not Fair!

Jackie didn't like being called names, and he didn't like being treated unfairly just because of the colour of his skin. He hated the way he and his friends were not allowed to swim in the public pool except on Tuesdays—the day before the water was changed. On hot summer days, they would gather outside the picket fence and watch the white kids splashing around in the water.

As a young teen, Jackie joined some neighbourhood kids in forming the Pepper Street Gang. They had decided to form a gang because they were angry at the way African American, Mexican, and Japanese kids were treated unfairly.

However, through his mother's strong family values and the influence of his coaches, Jackie realized that the Pepper Street Gang was no more than a ticket to trouble. He had the courage to quit the gang and decided to focus his efforts on sports.

Jackie was inspired by his big brother Mack, who was a U.S. Olympic athlete at the 1936 games held in Berlin, Germany.

All-Star Athlete

Jackie was filled with grief. His brother Frank had been killed in an accident. To take his mind off his grief, Jackie concentrated even harder on being the best he could be in sports. He began attending classes at the University of California in Los Angeles (UCLA). Soon, he was UCLA's best-known sports star.

Jackie trained hard, and he learned the importance of *discipline* and hard work. By focusing on sports, he was able to get through the tough times.

discipline strict training to improve performance and self-control

14

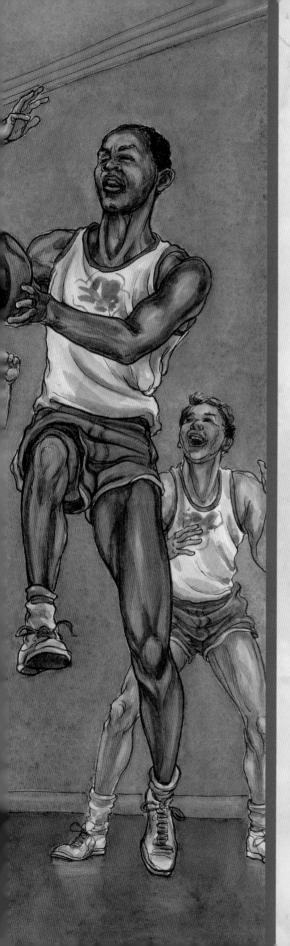

Jackie was a natural-born athlete, and throughout his college years he became a champion in track and field, football, basketball, and baseball.

Whenever Jackie came up against prejudice, he learned to turn the anger he felt into competitive energy.

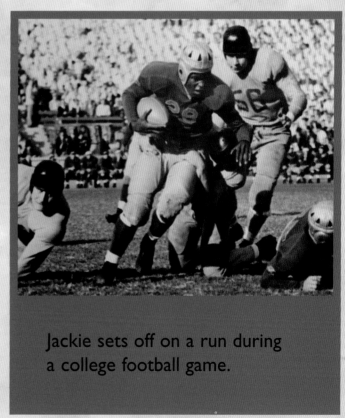

Jackie sets off on a run during a college football game.

The Big Break

"I want you to come and play for us."

Jackie couldn't believe his ears. Branch Rickey, one of the most important men in baseball, wanted him to play for his team! No major-league club had ever before hired a black ballplayer.

Rickey leaned forward. "At first, you'll be the only black player in the major league. Many people will be against you because of the colour of your skin. Can you take it?"

"Mr. Rickey, do you want a ballplayer who's afraid to fight back?" Jackie asked.

"I want a player with guts enough not to fight back," said Rickey.

Like other black ballplayers, Jackie had joined the separate league for African American players. Although there were many talented players in the all-black leagues, racism kept those players from joining the major all-white baseball teams.

Branch Rickey decided it was time that someone was brave enough to change this. He asked Jackie Robinson to play for the Montreal Royals.

Jackie and Branch Rickey shake hands after agreeing on a contract.

racism the belief that people of certain races are better than others

Keeping Cool

Jackie stood strong and tall beneath the bright lights of the New Jersey stadium. Playing in the Canadian league for the Montreal Royals was a big step forward. He was not about to let other people's prejudices ruin his baseball career. The crowd was mostly silent, but Jackie thought he could hear some booing. He held firm, however. Then and there, he decided that the best way to fight back was to play better than anyone else ever had.

Jackie kept his eye on the ball.

*"By giving in to
my feelings then,
I could have blown the
whole major league bit.
I swallowed my pride
and choked back
my anger."*
—Jackie R.

Many people dream of what it must be like to play a sport in a huge stadium full of cheering fans. For Jackie, this was a very different experience. Instead of cheers and praise, Jackie received hate mail and death threats. His wife and family were insulted, too. It was the hardest thing of all for Jackie to keep his cool and do nothing to defend himself.

Jackie withstood the pressure. Here he is congratulated by his teammates after making a home run.

Leading the Way

Jackie was true to his word. He ignored the hateful
things people said about him. He simply kept on
hitting the ball, stealing bases, and racing home
to win, win, win for his team.

In time, people began to respect his courage,
perseverance, and talent. They saw how Jackie
always did his best, even in a bad situation.
They saw past the colour of his skin,
and slowly began to change the way
they thought about African
American people.

perseverance not giving up

"I'm not concerned with your liking me or disliking me ... All I ask is that you respect me as a human being."
—Jackie R.

Jackie won many awards during his time in the big leagues. After his first year, two other African American players were signed to play major-league baseball, along with others in basketball and football.

Jackie had broken down unfair social barriers and opened up opportunities for other athletes of colour to play on professional teams. He changed North American sports forever.

Jackie (second from left) and his Brooklyn Dodgers teammates celebrate a win in 1951.

Fields of the Future

When Jackie Robinson retired from baseball after
ten years in the major leagues, he went on to speak
up for civil rights everywhere. He worked hard
to change the way people thought and to make life
better for others, and he did this in a nonviolent way.
Because of the courage, dignity, and commitment
he showed, Jackie Robinson became much more
than a sports champion—he became a hero.

commitment   being involved wholeheartedly

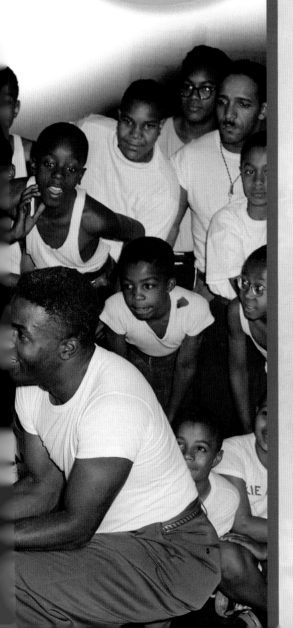

Civil Rights

Many people have worked hard to help change unfair situations and bring about equal rights for all. They often had to stand alone and go against the crowd to fight for what they believed in.

Jackie Robinson helped pave the way for other great leaders in the battle for civil rights. He worked with Dr. Martin Luther King, Jr. and the Reverend Jesse Jackson to help change society in a nonviolent way.

Jackie Robinson (right) with Martin Luther King, Jr.

23

More to Explore

1 Jackie Robinson had both talent and determination. In your opinion, which quality helped him the most in his career?

2 Find out why laws against segregation were finally passed in the United States.

Trailblazer means *the first one to do something.* Why is it usually hard to be a trailblazer?

Index